12 HEALTHY
HABITS FOR LIFE

by Carol Hand

12 STORY LIBRARY

www.12StoryLibrary.com

Copyright © 2017 by Peterson Publishing Company, North Mankato, MN 56003. All rights reserved. No part of this book may be reproduced or utilized in any form or by any means without written permission from the publisher.

12-Story Library is an imprint of Peterson Publishing Company and Press Room Editions.

Produced for 12-Story Library by Red Line Editorial

Photographs ©: michaeljung/Shutterstock Images, cover, 1; Nitr/Shutterstock Images, 4; Nathan Marx/iStockphoto, 5; Image Point Fr/Shutterstock Images, 6; shakzu/iStockphoto, 7; Steve Debenport/iStockphoto, 8; fotografixx/iStockphoto, 9; enciktat/Shutterstock Images, 10; MachineHeadz/iStockphoto, 11; Fertnig/iStockphoto, 12; szefei/iStockphoto, 13; monkeybusinessimages/iStockphoto/Thinkstock, 14; Blacqbook/iStockphoto, 15; Shantell/iStockphoto, 16; Khakimullin Aleksandr/Shutterstock Images, 17; hxdbzxy/Shutterstock Images, 18; Piotr Marcinski/Shutterstock Images, 19; alysta/Shutterstock Images, 20, 29; Pakphoto/iStockphoto, 21; Dean Mitchell/iStockphoto, 22, 28; paulaphoto/Shutterstock Images, 23; Maridav/iStockphoto, 24; wavebreakmedia/Shutterstock Images, 25; Mandy Godbehear/Shutterstock Images, 26; Christopher Edwin Nuzzaco/Shutterstock Images, 27

Library of Congress Cataloging-in-Publication Data
Cataloging-in-publication information is on file with the Library of Congress.
978-1-63235-364-1 (hardcover)
978-1-63235-382-5 (paperback)
978-1-62143-506-8 (hosted ebook)

Printed in the United States of America
Mankato, MN
May, 2017

Table of Contents

Create a Healthy Diet to Increase Energy 4

Read Food Labels 6

Swap Out Caffeinated, Sugary Drinks 8

Spend Time with Friends to Build Social Skills 10

Limit Screen Time 12

Find Fun Ways to Exercise 14

Sleep Well to Recharge Your Body 16

Build Better Health with Good Hygiene 18

Be Prepared and Be Safe 20

Read to Gain Knowledge and Self-Respect 22

Soothe Stress in Nature 24

Stay Positive to Lead a Happy Life 26

Fact Sheet 28

Glossary 30

For More Information 31

Index 32

About the Author 32

Create a Healthy Diet to Increase Energy

Good habits keep people healthy and happy. It is important to develop good habits early in life. This way, habits become natural. Healthy eating is a good habit. It gives you energy to think and play. It also helps you concentrate, sleep better, and feel better.

Foods provide energy. Energy is measured in calories. People who eat too many calories store them as fat. People who eat too few calories are tired. They lack energy. The kind of calories you eat also matters. Healthy foods provide chemicals called nutrients. Bodies need nutrients to grow and work properly. Calcium builds strong bones and teeth. Protein builds muscle. Iron helps make red blood cells, which carry oxygen through the body.

Eat fresh fruit in place of desserts such as cakes and pies, which are high in sugars and fats.

A person must eat a variety of foods to get all the nutrients needed for good health. This is a healthy, balanced diet.

Healthy meals are colorful. Colorful vegetables and fruits have many nutrients. They have low or no fat and few calories. They also have fiber, which makes it easy to digest food. Half of each meal should be bright-colored vegetables, such as peas, broccoli, carrots, and tomatoes.

A good diet also includes meats, eggs, and dairy products. It includes legumes such as beans and peas. All of these foods are rich in protein. Whole grain breads, pastas, cereals, and small amounts of oil are also important. A mixture of all these foods keeps people healthy.

Eating a healthy, balanced diet keeps the body energized for physical activity.

2,000
Average number of calories an active person age 9 to 13 should consume each day.

- People should develop healthy eating habits when young.
- Healthy foods provide energy needed for activity.
- Healthy foods provide the nutrients that bodies need to grow and work properly.
- A variety of foods, including many vegetables and fruits, make up a balanced diet.

THINK ABOUT IT

Plan a day's meals following the rules in this section. How colorful can you make your meals? Is this plan similar to what you usually eat? How could you improve your food choices?

Read Food Labels

How do you know which foods and drinks are healthy? Any packaged food has a "Nutrition Facts" label. This label breaks down the amount

of each nutrient in the food. Always check the serving size, which is often smaller than the package size. If you eat a two-ounce (56.7 g) bag of chips, and the serving size is one ounce (28.3 g), you will eat twice the calories and nutrients listed on the label.

The percentage of each nutrient, vitamin, and mineral is also listed on a food label. A food with five percent or less of a substance is a poor source. A food with a 10 to 20 percent level is a good source. A food with more than 20 percent is high in that substance.

Food labels list ingredients in order of amounts present in the food. Most of the food consists of the first ingredient. For example, a can of tuna should have tuna as the first ingredient. To make a habit of picking healthy foods, look for good or high sources of substances you

Make reading food labels a habit to learn more about what you are putting into your body.

25% • Pantothenic Acid 25% • Phosphorus 20
num 35%

)GE (CORN SYRUP, INVERT SUGAR, PEANUT BUTTER [PEANUT
ROB SEED GUM, BETA-CAROTENE), CHOCOLATE FLAVORED CC
FLAVOR), CORN SYRUP, ACACIA GUM, FRUCTOSE SYRUP, PE,
PHOSPHATE, SALT, **VITAMIN AND MINERAL BLEND** (CALCIUI
ROUS FUMARATE, PYRIDOXINE HYDROCHLORIDE, VITAMIN A PAI
AMIN).
:S EGGS, TREE NUTS AND WHEAT.

Learn the sugar lingo so you can choose better foods.

need, such as protein or fiber. Look for small amounts of sugar, fat, and sodium, which is salt.

2,000
Number of calories in the diet on which food label percentages are based.

- The Nutrition Facts label lists the type and amount of nutrients.
- Percentages tell if a food is a poor, good, or high source of an ingredient.
- The food label lists nutrients according to amounts contained within the product.
- Avoid packaged foods high in sugar, sodium, and fat.

HIDDEN SUGARS

Foods can contain more than 50 forms of sugar. Often, the ingredients list contains several of them. Some of the hidden sugars to watch for include sucrose, fructose, lactose, or any other word ending in -ose. Also watch for syrups, especially high-fructose corn syrup (HFCS). HFCS is similar to sucrose (table sugar) and is added to many foods. Eating too much of any sugar is linked to weight gain and heart disease.

Swap Out Caffeinated, Sugary Drinks

Soft drinks, or sodas, can taste delicious, but they are unhealthy. Sodas have high levels of sugar and caffeine. Sugar and caffeine provide a burst of energy that only lasts approximately an hour. Sodas cause the body to store extra sugar as fat. This causes weight gain. The sugar in soda can lead to diseases, including diabetes and heart disease. The acid and sugar both cause tooth decay.

The healthiest drink is water, so a healthy habit to develop is to drink mostly water. Water has no sugar, caffeine, or calories. It makes up 60 percent of our body weight. It keeps our body temperatures constant. We use water for all body

The caffeine in sodas and energy drinks tricks the brain into feeling pleasure, which can form an addiction.

functions. Water also moves nutrients and oxygen to body cells and removes wastes. Other healthy drinks are milks, unsweetened fruit juices, and vegetable drinks, such as tomato juice. Try to limit the fruit juices. Although they have many nutrients, they are also high in sugar. Drinks to avoid include sodas, energy drinks, flavored milks, and sweet tea.

8

Number of glasses of water a 9-to-13 year old should drink every day.

- Drinking sodas and other drinks high in sugar and caffeine can lead to addiction and obesity.
- Sodas and sugary drinks increase tooth decay.
- Water is the healthiest drink choice. The body needs it for all bodily functions.

SODAS AND OBESITY

Some overweight children in the United States drink 1,000 to 2,000 calories of sodas every day. Sodas lack the nutrients the body needs. Dr. Marion Nestle, a professor of nutrition, says, "The first thing that anyone should do if they are trying to lose weight is to eliminate or cut down on soft drinks."

4

Spend Time with Friends to Build Social Skills

Nearly everyone enjoys hanging out with friends. It's an excellent habit to build into a healthy life. Spending time with friends helps build social skills. Social skills help us get along with others. They make us better friends. As you talk with friends, you learn to communicate better.

You can develop social skills by following a three-step program:

see, think, and do. Seeing involves watching for clues about how another person feels. Good friends observe their friends. They notice how friends act and respond. They respect people's feelings.

Friends also think about why people respond as they do. They ask themselves: Is my friend comfortable with my behavior? Do I annoy her or

Talking with friends helps teach you to be a member of a group.

hurt her feelings? With practice, you can tell if a person is happy, sad, or angry by watching facial expressions and actions. You can predict how your friend will react in certain situations.

The third step is doing. If you see that your behavior is upsetting, you can change it. For example, you might stop teasing, or stop talking and listen to the other person. And don't forget the social skills you learned as a young child. Saying "thank you" shows that you are grateful. Smiling shows pleasure and can lift another person's spirits. Be patient. Wait in line or let others go first. This shows concern and

respect. Connecting by smartphone is fine sometimes. The best way to develop good social skills is by hanging out with friends in person.

33
Percent fewer errors in reading emotions after five days away from screens.

- Social skills, such as having good manners, make people better friends.
- Good social skills result from practice.
- Screen time limits your ability to develop social skills.

Texting and communicating through other forms of technology can limit your ability to develop social skills.

Limit Screen Time

Screens are everywhere—on TVs, computers, tablets, and smartphones, just to name a few. How much time do you spend in front of screens each day? The average child spends five to seven hours every day in front of a screen. A healthy habit to develop is to limit your screen time.

Screen activities are fun, but they can become addictive. Some people spend too much time sitting in front of a screen. People are not active while sitting in front of a screen. They often eat unhealthy snacks while watching TV or gaming. For these reasons, too much screen time can cause obesity. At the same time, people's senses can become overstimulated. This can cause them to have trouble paying attention and even sleeping.

Of course, this doesn't mean you have to stop using your smartphone, tablet, or computer. In fact, computers and tablets can be a great help when it comes to researching for homework. The important thing is to limit your screen time. Schedule short screen

Sitting in front of a screen makes it easy to be inactive and snack on unhealthy foods.

times. When the scheduled time is over, turn the screen off. And be sure to choose appropriate games and shows.

Doctors recommend two hours or less per day of screen time for all kids over the age of two. This leaves more time for fun activities. It means more time for sports, reading, active play, and spending time with friends and family.

Some screen time is good as long as it is limited.

HOW SCREEN TIME CHANGES THE BRAIN

Doctors have done brain scans to test how brains change when exposed to screen time. At first, brain changes are small. They become more noticeable as screen time increases. Changes are most noticeable in people with screen addictions. The thinking and planning parts of the brain shrink in size. Areas that block bad behavior and help people have sympathy for others also shrink. This damage makes people less able to communicate with others.

2

Age by which most children begin using tablets and smartphones in the United States.

- Too much screen time can cause obesity and attention problems.
- Limit screen time to approximately two hours per day or less.
- Less screen time means more time for other activities.

13

Find Fun Ways to Exercise

Being active is one of the best habits to develop. Physical activity helps control body weight. People who exercise have more energy. They feel better about themselves and are more self-confident. They even live longer than those who don't exercise.

Exercise is so great for the body because it keeps the heart and blood vessels healthy. When people are inactive and become overweight, fat can enter the blood. It then attaches to blood vessel walls. This raises blood pressure and can cause heart attacks. Regular exercise prevents these problems. It speeds up blood flow. It flushes fat from the blood vessels. It even helps bring oxygen to your body's cells.

We all need at least 60 minutes of moderate to vigorous activity

Getting in your day's worth of activity could be as simple as biking with friends or family.

Swimming is an aerobic exercise that is fun and doesn't have to be competitive.

daily. Rapid walking is an example of moderate activity. Jogging or bicycling fast are examples of vigorous activity. The activity should be aerobic. This means it should raise heart and breathing rates.

Daily exercise does not have to be done all at once. It might be two 30-minute periods or four 15-minute periods.

FUN AEROBIC EXERCISES

Aerobic exercise includes games or activities that involve brisk walking or running. Gymnastics, playing on a jungle gym, and climbing trees are also aerobic. Doing push-ups and jumping rope are excellent activities. Sports such as swimming, basketball, and soccer all involve healthy aerobic exercises. Learning healthy exercises and making exercise a habit lead to a healthier life.

12,000
Average number of steps a person 6 to 17 years old should take each day.

- Being active makes a person healthier and more self-confident.
- You should get 60 minutes of moderate activity every day.
- Activity should be aerobic, increasing heart and breathing rates.
- Walking, running, and gymnastics are all good aerobic activities.

Build Better Health with Good Hygiene

Hygiene includes all the habits people develop to keep themselves clean. Everyone gets dirty. This is normal, so washing is important. Germs are all around us. Bacteria and viruses can cause infections, such as colds and flu. Washing gets rids of germs that you pick up in your daily activities. It is important to wash your hands several times a day. This includes scrubbing under your nails.

Body and hair washing are also important for hygiene. Taking a regular bath or shower is a good habit to develop. If you are extremely active or around crowds or sick people, daily showers are a good idea. But with normal activity, every second or third day is fine. Fewer baths or showers will keep your skin soft and prevent it from drying

Wash your hands before eating, after using the toilet, after physical activity that may make you dirty or sweaty, and after handling dirty objects or uncooked foods.

out. When washing the body, be sure to wash under your arms and under your nails. Bacteria collect in the underarms and can get lodged underneath nails that are not trimmed or scrubbed. Wash your hair every other day, or whenever it gets dirty.

Another important hygiene habit is brushing your teeth. Brushing and flossing teeth removes food particles from your mouth that could break down and lead to cavities. It also prevents bad breath. Good hygiene makes people healthier and makes them feel better. It also makes them more pleasant to be around!

20
Number of seconds it takes to wash hands thoroughly.

- Washing hands after activities involving dirt or germs prevents disease.
- Washing the body regularly is necessary for good hygiene.
- Brushing and flossing your teeth at least twice per day keeps your mouth healthy.
- Clean hair, fingernails, and underarms are important for good hygiene.

Dentists suggest brushing and flossing your teeth at least twice a day or after every meal.

Be Prepared and Be Safe

Being safe is a healthy habit. Injuries can happen if you are not alert to possible dangers. Occasional scrapes and bruises are part of everyday life. But awareness and preparation can help you prevent serious injuries and keep you safe.

Deep water in pools or lakes is one possible danger. The first rule of water safety is to learn to swim. Take swimming lessons or have someone teach you. Always make sure a lifeguard or other adult is present and always swim with a buddy. Never swim alone. If there is an emergency, immediately find an adult or call 911.

There are also important safety rules for traveling in a vehicle. Make it a habit to buckle up every time you get in a vehicle. Seatbelts are not just for long trips. Wearing a seatbelt in the car is a key safety rule. It is also the law. If you are walking somewhere, always follow rules for safely crossing the street.

Wear a life vest whenever taking part in water sports.

STAY SAFE AROUND STRANGERS

It's also important to be aware of dangers from other people. Stay away from strangers who invite you to go somewhere or offer you something. Quickly run to a safe place and tell a trusted adult. Strangers can threaten you online, too. Cyberbullying occurs when another person threatens or scares you online. If an online stranger tries to meet you, let an adult know right away. Also stop communicating with that person. Stay safe by learning about online dangers and following the guidelines set up by adults. If someone threatens you—either online or in person— immediately tell a parent or trusted adult.

Always wear a helmet when biking or skateboarding. Ride only in daylight and never ride alone.

911

Emergency number to call in most locations.

- Avoid injuries by being prepared and staying aware of your surroundings.
- Have adult supervision to stay safe around water.
- Follow safety rules for crossing streets.
- Always use safety equipment, including helmets and seatbelts.

Buckle up each time you get into a vehicle.

Read to Gain Knowledge and Self-Respect

Reading is a healthy habit that can benefit you on many levels. There are two types of stories or books: fiction and nonfiction. Fiction is about imaginary characters. Nonfiction is about real people and information. Reading fictional stories sparks imagination. Stories about characters and their adventures

and struggles help us understand ourselves and others. Reading nonfiction gives us information. It helps us understand the world and how it works.

People read fiction for the same reasons they see a good movie. Reading is great entertainment. It shows how other people respond

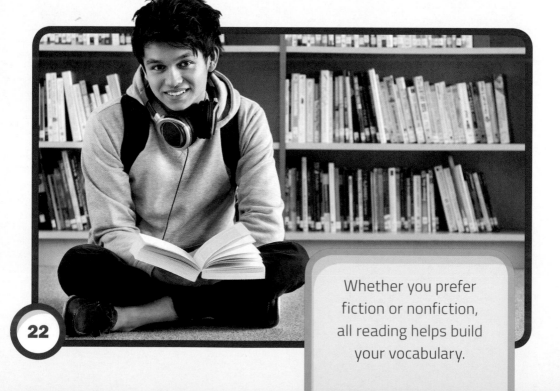

Whether you prefer fiction or nonfiction, all reading helps build your vocabulary.

Trying reading something for fun.

to events. It allows readers to experience other parts of the world and other kinds of life.

Reading nonfiction can teach you about anything that interests you. From insects to rockets, from history to heroes—the whole world is open to nonfiction readers. People also read to prepare for their futures. People read textbooks and articles about how to be a doctor. Car lovers read car magazines and books about how engines work.

As with any habit, practice makes perfect. Reading more makes you a stronger reader. Stronger readers tend to be happier people. Why? Studies show that readers have higher self-esteem than those who don't read. They respect themselves more. Reading helps improve concentration and memory. Reading is an active skill. It exercises the brain and teaches problem solving.

50,000
Average number of words in the vocabulary of a typical high-school graduate.

- Reading improves brain function and self-esteem.
- Reading fiction expands our imaginations.
- Reading nonfiction helps us learn new information.

Soothe Stress in Nature

Today, many people see nature mostly on television shows. They can identify animals and describe a forest. But the most important benefit of nature is not facts. It is the improved physical and mental health and positive emotions people can feel when in nature.

Nature is where humans developed and learned to survive. Studies show that we still need to spend time in nature to develop and be healthy.

When you play outdoors, without adults or structured activities, you learn to pay attention to things around you and solve problems on your own. You feel better and have more self-respect. Carving out time for nature is a healthy habit for life. Nature soothes and restores people of all ages.

Being in nature is harder now than it was when your parents and grandparents were young. Natural

In nature, stress can melt away and your mood can improve.

If you live in the city, see if there are gardens or other outdoor activities you can take part in.

areas are harder to find. Cell phones and video games distract you. Nevertheless, nature is still all around us. Cities have parks filled with plants and animals. Schools might have gardens. Look for nature trails you can hike or explore a new bike path. Visit a zoo and watch the animals. Visit a planetarium and look at the stars. Be aware of the changing seasons and play outdoors in the snow and rain. Have picnics or camp in natural areas. Just enjoy being outdoors. Finding ways to experience nature regularly is a healthy habit to develop.

411
Number of areas included in the US national park system.

- Kids today spend far less time in nature than their parents and grandparents did.
- Nature experiences improve the body, mind, and emotions.
- They relieve stress and improve mood.
- City kids can experience nature in parks, gardens, zoos, and backyards.

THINK ABOUT IT

Describe how a special outdoor experience made you feel. Or describe an outdoor experience you would like to have.

Stay Positive to Lead a Happy Life

A person's attitude, or the way he or she thinks and feels about things, has a big effect on his or her life. Looking for the best in life helps people enjoy the good times. It makes them stronger and helps them meet challenges when things go wrong. It cuts down on worry and stress.

People cannot always control what happens in life. But they can control how they react to events. Experts say you can do this by paying attention to your thoughts. Try to change a negative thought into a positive thought. With practice, this can become a habit. Instead of giving up, believe you can handle problems and things will eventually get better. Don't keep your worries all to yourself. Share your fears with parents, other caring adults, and friends. Find out how they cope with problems and keep good attitudes.

Other simple tools to develop a positive attitude include finding ways

Find healthy ways to let go of your stress.

- A positive attitude can improve a person's life.
- Positive people try to solve problems instead of ignoring them.
- Learn simple tools to control and contribute to your positive attitude.

to have fun. Watch a fun movie or spend time with friends. Laughing actually helps people feel better. Also, let go of anger. If someone makes you angry, try to respond by doing or saying something nice. Always be kind to people. Practice thinking about how other people are feeling. Have sympathy for their problems. Smile at them or give them a compliment.

Finally, keep a journal of things you do and things that happen to you. When something bad happens, write it down and think about it. What can you learn from this experience? How can you keep it from happening again? When you read it over a week later, does it still seem as important? Having a positive attitude will help form all of your healthy habits.

Journaling can help you reflect on and learn from your feelings and experiences.

Fact Sheet

- Many foods help prevent disease, as well as build strong, healthy bodies. Orange and dark green vegetables, such as carrots, sweet potatoes, spinach, and kale, contain a chemical called beta carotene. The body changes this chemical to vitamin A. Vitamin A, plus vitamins C and E, helps protect vision. Foods high in fiber, such as whole grains, improve digestion by helping move food through the digestive tract. This decreases digestive problems. Fibrous vegetables such as beans remove cholesterol from the bloodstream, helping prevent heart disease. Spicy foods such as chili cause membranes of the nose and throat to produce a watery liquid. This makes it easier to remove mucus when you have a cold.

- Many of the healthy habits in this book can help avoid Internet addiction. An Internet-addicted person spends a lot of time online, loses track of time while online, sleeps with his or her smartphone on, chooses Internet activity over being with friends, and feels uncomfortable away from his or her smartphone or tablet. Internet addiction causes visible changes in the brain.

When a brain area is used less, it decreases in size, just as unused muscles do. One such area is the frontal lobe (just behind the forehead). This area controls functions related to productivity, such as planning and organizing. Internet-addicted people do fewer tasks involving thinking. Another damaged area, called the insula, is involved in the ability to develop compassion, or sympathy, for others. It helps us link physical signs with emotions. Damage to this area affects personal relationships.

Glossary

addiction
A very strong habit in which a person becomes dependent on something; for example, a sugar addiction.

aerobic activity
Activity intense enough to increase heart and breathing rates; activity that improves circulation and general body condition.

attitude
The way a person thinks or feels about something; for example, having a positive attitude about life.

caffeine
A chemical found in coffee, tea, and most soda drinks that stimulates or arouses the body.

calories
The unit used to measure the amount of energy in food.

immune system
The body system that protects the body from disease and keeps you from getting sick.

nonfiction
Writing based on facts or information; writing designed to provide knowledge.

obesity
Having too much body fat for good health; condition of being very overweight.

self-esteem
Having respect for oneself or feeling good about oneself.

For More Information

Books

Bellisario, Gina. *Keep Calm!: My Stress-Busting Tips.* Minneapolis, MN: Millbrook Press, 2014.

Meiners, Cheri J. *Grow Strong! A Book about Healthy Habits.* Minneapolis, MN: Free Spirit Publishing, 2016.

Sjonger, Rebecca. *Stress Less!: A Kid's Guide to Managing Emotions.* New York: Crabtree Publishing, 2016.

Visit 12StoryLibrary.com

Scan the code or use your school's login at **12StoryLibrary.com** for recent updates about this topic and a full digital version of this book. Enjoy free access to:

- Digital ebook
- Breaking news updates
- Live content feeds
- Videos, interactive maps, and graphics
- Additional web resources

Note to educators: Visit 12StoryLibrary.com/register to sign up for free premium website access. Enjoy live content plus a full digital version of every 12-Story Library book you own for every student at your school.

Index

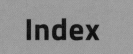

aerobic activity, 15
attitude, 26–27

brain, 13, 16, 17, 23

caffeine, 8, 9, 17
calcium, 4
calories, 4–5, 6, 7, 8, 9
communication, 10, 13, 21

diet, 4–5, 7

energy, 4–5, 8–9, 14
exercise, 14–15, 17, 23

food labels, 6–7

hygiene, 18–19

nature, 24–25
nutrients, 4–5, 6–7, 9

obesity, 9, 12, 13

preparedness, 20–21, 23
protein, 4–5, 7

reading, 6–7, 11, 13, 17, 22–23, 27

safety, 20–21
screen time, 11, 12–13
self-respect, 24
sleep, 4, 12, 16–17
social skills, 10–11, 12–13
strangers, 21
stress, 24–25, 26
sugar, 7, 8–9, 17

water, 8–9, 20, 21

About the Author

Carol Hand is a freelance science writer who has authored more than 30 science and health books for young people. She is trained in zoology and has taught college biology and developed science curricula.

READ MORE FROM 12-STORY LIBRARY

Every 12-Story Library book is available in many formats. For more information, visit 12StoryLibrary.com.